Lucia Clark is a Partner in the Family Law team at Morton Fraser in Edinburgh. An accredited Scottish family law specialist and mediator, she has particular expertise in resolving complex financial disputes. She is frequently sought out in cases involving high-value assets such as businesses or farms, and in cases with an international aspect. Lucia has considerable experience and interest in the niche area of farming divorce, and frequently advises farmers or spouses on the particular issues faced by them on relationship breakdown. Consistently highly rated in the legal directories, she was described in Chambers 2020/2021 as "massively intelligent" and in Chambers 2021/22 as "down to earth and measured with clients".

A Practical Guide to Divorce and Farming in Scotland

A Practical Guide to Divorce and Farming in Scotland

Lucia Clark
Partner, Morton Fraser LLP
LLB (Hons)

Law Brief Publishing

© Lucia Clark

All rights reserved. No part of this publication may be reproduced, stored in a retrieval system, or transmitted, in any form or by any means, electronic, mechanical, photocopying, recording or otherwise, without the prior permission of the publisher.

Excerpts from judgments and statutes are Crown copyright. Any Crown Copyright material is reproduced with the permission of the Controller of OPSI and the Queen's Printer for Scotland. Some quotations may be licensed under the terms of the Open Government Licence (http://www.nationalarchives.gov.uk/doc/open-government-licence/version/3).

Cover image © iStockphoto.com/mrdoomits

The information in this book was believed to be correct at the time of writing. All content is for information purposes only and is not intended as legal advice. No liability is accepted by either the publisher or author for any errors or omissions (whether negligent or not) that it may contain. Professional advice should always be obtained before applying any information to particular circumstances.

Published 2022 by Law Brief Publishing, an imprint of Law Brief Publishing Ltd
30 The Parks
Minehead
Somerset
TA24 8BT

www.lawbriefpublishing.com

Paperback: 978-1-914608-12-4

PREFACE

As you, the reader, will be quite aware from the title, this is a guide to a rather niche area of family law. As such, it is assumed that the reader already has a working knowledge of the Family Law (Scotland) Act 1985, and not every concept or definition from that Act will be covered in detail.

Whilst this text will cover a range of areas less familiar to the family lawyer – property and partnerships in particular – it is not to be taken as a suggestion or recommendation that the family lawyer proceed entirely by themselves in farming divorce cases, without the assistance of specialist advice in those areas. It is intended as a general guide, to alert the family lawyer to areas to be aware of, rather than a substitute for bringing in property, corporate, tax or other colleagues and experts as needed.

Writing this book has been a thoroughly – perhaps surprisingly – enjoyable experience, but it is not one I could have done without considerable help. I would wish to thank my colleagues at Morton Fraser, Douglas Milne, Alistair Anderson and Adrian Bell for their guidance on planning, agricultural and corporate law respectively; and Rhona Adams and Anna Maitles for being encouraging "first readers" from family law. Last, but by no means least, Ewan, Lewis and Fiona, for being precisely no help with any legal research or drafting, but being invaluable in every way that actually matters. And sorry, despite your suggestions that I "add some dragons or wizards to make it more interesting", I didn't quite manage to fit them in.

The law quoted in this edition is accurate as at 31 October 2021.

Lucia Clark
November 2021

CONTENTS

Chapter One	Overview – What Makes a Farming Divorce Complex?	1
Chapter Two	The First Meeting	5
Chapter Three	The Farm Business – Partnerships	11
	What is a partnership?	11
	Is the partnership interest matrimonial?	12
	Pre-marital acquisition	12
	Acquisition by way of gift or inheritance	14
	Increase in value of the capital account	16
Chapter Four	The Farm Business – Other Business Entities	19
	Sole traders	19
	Companies	20
Chapter Five	The Farmland	23
	What land is owned?	23
	Who is the landowner?	24
	Who occupies the land?	25
	What restrictions are there about use of the land?	25
	Is there a security over the land?	26
	Is the land matrimonial property?	27
	Was the land gifted?	27
	What about a house built on non-matrimonial land?	30
Chapter Six	Is the Farmland Within the Partnership?	33
	Land bought with partnership funds	33
	Land acquired for the purposes of partnership business	35
Chapter Seven	Interaction of Matrimonial and Partnership Law	41
	Orders for transfer of an interest in a partnership	41
	Transfer or sale of partnership assets	42
	Preventing dissolution	43
	Varying the terms of a partnership agreement	44

Chapter Eight	Other Farming Assets and Diversification	47
	Subsidies	47
	Renewable energy	48
	Radio masts	49
	Planning and development	49
	Wayleaves	51
	Holiday lets	51
	Leases of equipment	51
	Natural capital	51
	Forests and fishing	52
Chapter Nine	Getting Valuations and Expert Advice	53
	General issues for valuations	53
	Date of valuation	56
	The land valuer	57
	The stock, subsidy and machinery valuers	58
	The accountants	59
	The tax expert	60
Chapter Ten	Arguing Unequal Division	61
	Special circumstances	61
	Economic disadvantage and burden of childcare	63
Chapter Eleven	Arguing Lack of Resources	67
	Sale of the land	67
	Borrowing	68
Chapter Twelve	Dealing With the Farm Partnership	71
	Dissolution of the partnership	71
	Transfer of one partner's share	73
	Continuation of the partnership	74
Chapter Thirteen	Dealing With Family Dynamics	75
Chapter Fourteen	Preventative Steps	79
	Pre- and post-nuptial agreements	79
	Partnership agreements	81
Chapter Fifteen	Tips for Farm Advisers	83

CHAPTER ONE

OVERVIEW – WHAT MAKES A FARMING DIVORCE COMPLEX?

Scottish family lawyers are all familiar with the basic law regarding financial provision on divorce, as set out in the Family Law (Scotland) Act 1985 ("the 1985 Act") and the relevant case law. So what makes farming divorce different from any other marital breakdown, such as to distinguish this book from the many excellent guides to the 1985 Act already available?

First, it is often particularly complex in farming cases to distinguish what is matrimonial property and what isn't. Getting the case off on the right foot is essential in this regard, and Chapter Two covers practical suggestions for the first meeting and information gathering. Chapters Three to Six then go on to examine in detail, with regard to the caselaw, how to consider whether both the land and the farm business are matrimonial property; and also whether the land is held within the business or not. The nuances of partnership law can be unfamiliar territory for family lawyers, but are often essential to understanding and disentangling what is and isn't matrimonial property in a farming dispute.

Second, a farming divorce often involves advising on two separate but related disputes – the matrimonial claims between spouses and also the business-related claims between the partners in the farming business. Sometimes, the spouses and business partners are the same people; sometimes, others will be involved in the farm business, and more often than not, these are other family members. Those family members may be the older generation, or the younger generation, or the siblings of one spouse. This gives an extra dimension to the dispute which will often makes things far more difficult to resolve, particularly for family lawyers used to dealing with litigation involving only two parties. The issues arising from partnership claims and family dynamics are examined in Chapters Seven, Twelve and Thirteen.

Third, the fact that the farmland and business is very often gifted or inherited places a particularly urgent focus on arguments for unequal division. For the claimant, that tends to mean claims for "economic disadvantage" if the bulk of the wealth has remained non-matrimonial; for the farmer, it will likely mean increased importance for source of funds arguments, if there has been conversion from gift/inheritance to matrimonial property. These are covered in Chapter Ten.

Fourth, the particular nature of farm assets means that frequently, there is little in the way of liquid assets; sometimes, all or almost all of the wealth is tied up in the farmland and business. A general reluctance to sell land can lead to detailed arguments about lack of resources, covered in Chapter Eleven.

Lastly, we turn to look at preventative steps in Chapters Fourteen and Fifteen – how farmers (assisted by their advisers and accountants) can try to avoid getting into a lengthy and complex litigated divorce disputes. In retrospect and once a marriage has broken down, helpful "tax savings" prompted by advisers to bring a spouse into the partnership, or put assets into the spouse's name, can seem like disastrous financial advice; and planning a more detailed partnership or pre-nuptial agreement a much better idea.

Clearly, farmers can be both men and women, and I will avoid referring to the farmer as "he" or the spouse as "she" (or vice versa). Again, both spouses may be equal owners of the land, and equally involved in the farm business. However, it is more common for the land to have been passed down through one spouse's family, or otherwise acquired by that spouse. I will therefore refer to one spouse as the "farmer" meaning the main owner of the land, or main person involved in the farm business. I will refer to the other spouse as the "claimant".

CHAPTER TWO

THE FIRST MEETING – FACT FINDING AND INFORMATION GATHERING

In all cases, the first meeting is particularly important in establishing a good working relationship between client and solicitor, and in setting the tone for moving forward. However, in farming divorce cases, it can be more difficult than usual at a first meeting to get a handle on the various aspects of the case, or to give a clear steer on parameters for a likely outcome.

This is both due to the complexities of the law as it applies to farming scenarios, and also due to difficulties in establishing the extent and nature of the assets. Farming clients can often be very clear about the practicalities of their day-to-day work, while considerably less clear about the legal niceties of title deeds or business arrangements. The solicitor's job is therefore to dig into these details, however unimportant the client may have thought them up to now, and seek to get documentation and other evidence to cross-check whether what the client thinks about land and business arrangements is actually correct.

This chapter is intended as a practical checklist of what questions to ask at, or shortly after, a first meeting. This are not intended to cover everything that the solicitor will need to know over the course of a farming divorce case – far from it – but to be a sound first starting point.

General aims:

- Where does the client want to be in a year's time? On the farm and involved in the business; or living elsewhere?

- Does the client see the farm business continuing, or the assets being sold?

- Does the client intend or wish the farm to pass to other family members in the future?

The business:

- How is the business set up? Is it a sole trader, partnership or company? Is there more than one business entity to cover different aspects of the farming business?

- Who is the business accountant or adviser? Is the client content for that accountant to be contacted directly for further details/documents?

- Does the client have copy accounts for the business? If not, who does? Can a run of accounts be provided, ideally covering the entire period from before the marriage to date? Who might have these?

- Did either spouse pay any consideration to acquire their respective stakes in the business? If so, when and to whom?

- Has there been (or is there any future possibility of) diversification e.g. wind turbines, holiday cottages, lease of farm machinery? If so, is that run through the same farm business, or separately?

If the business is a company:

- What is the exact company name and number? Does the client have basic company documentation, or should this be obtained from Companies House?

- Is there a shareholders agreement?

- Are there shareholders other than the spouses?

If the business is a partnership:

- How is the partnership established – general partnership, Limited Partnership, or LLP?

- Is there a written partnership agreement, and if so, who has a copy of this?

- When was the partnership constituted?

- Who are the other partners?

- Has there been any change to the partnership during the period of the marriage – e.g. new partners taken on, new partnership agreement signed?

The land

- What land is owned?

- Is all or any part of the farm rented and if so what is the nature of the tenancy?

- Who holds the titles? Can the client (or anyone else) provide copies, or does the Land Register or Sasines Register need to be checked?

- Whose name is on the title deeds? Is that the same or different to whom the client thinks the true owner of the land is (e.g. if the title deed in the name of individual(s) but the client believes the land is owned by the partnership)?

- Was any consideration of any kind made in exchange for the land acquisition (whether or not recorded on the title deed)?

- Does the client have any idea of the value of the land (and is that different from the current value per the accounts)?

- Is there any development potential for the land? If so, what?

Arguments

- Has the claimant contributed time and energy to the farm business or the family? If so, how? Have they given up the possibilities of a career or opportunities elsewhere? If so, what?

- Have there been any gifts or inheritances of land or other assets forming part of the farm? If a gift, is this documented? Is the giver still alive and could he/she provide a statement about this?

Resources

- Would the farm business be viable if part of the assets were sold?

- What other options might there be for raising money for a potential settlement?

- Is there any debt?

CHAPTER THREE

THE FARM BUSINESS – PARTNERSHIPS

In any farm, there will be a farm business. The type of business entity involved (or indeed types, as there may be more than one) and how this has been established will greatly impact on financial provision. Many farm businesses have, historically, been run as partnerships – perhaps the most difficult and ambiguous of the possible business entities to deal with on divorce.

<u>What is a partnership?</u>

Difficult as it may be to believe, partnerships in the UK continue to be regulated by the Partnership Act 1890, a piece of legislation now over 130 years old. Partnership is defined within that Act as *"the relation which subsists between persons carrying on a business in common with a view of profit"*. Unlike in England and Wales, in Scotland, per s4(2) of the Partnership Act, *"a firm is a legal person distinct from the partners of whom it is composed"*.

The 130-year-old default rules set out in the Partnership Act 1890 will, in the absence of any other agreement, continue to apply to regulate a partnership's dealings and dissolution. There may be a written partnership agreement. It is, unfortunately, fairly common to find farming partnerships which have been constituted orally and with no written documentation. If there is no written agreement, it is important to bear in mind that the relationship of partnership is based on *agreement* and it is possible to find the terms of the partnership in writings other than a formal agreement and in the actions of the partners (frequently evidenced by the accounts).

Is the partnership interest matrimonial?

The first question to ask is whether the farmer's interest in the farm partnership (and any interest of the claimant in the partnership if he/she has been assumed as a partner) falls within the definition of "matrimonial property" per the 1985 Act. Per Section 10(4) of the 1985 Act, "matrimonial property" means:

> *"all the property belonging to the parties or either of them at the relevant date which was acquired by them or him (otherwise than by way of gift or succession from a third party)—*
>
> > *(a) before the marriage for use by them as a family home or as furniture or plenishings for such home; or*
> >
> > *(b) during the marriage but before the relevant date."*

The farmer may well seek to argue that interest in the partnership was acquired pre-marriage, or inherited, or gifted. To investigate this, there are various issues to consider. These should be considered in conjunction with any Partnership Agreement, and (if at all possible) a run of the partnership accounts, from the period just prior to the marriage to date.

Pre-marital acquisition

The first, and obvious, question is when the partnership commenced – during the marriage, or prior to it? If the interest was acquired prior to the marriage, the view set out in a number of cases is that this will not constitute matrimonial property, if that interest has remained unchanged in form throughout the marriage, and subject to any potential arguments about retained profits (see section on "Increases in value within a capital account" below).

However, the date of acquisition of a partnership interest may not be immediately obvious. If so, useful places to investigate are the Partnership Agreement (if there is one), as that will often give a commencement date; the accounts; the views of the partners themselves; and the views of any business adviser/accountant. One example of ambiguity is set out in the Outer House judgment in *Jack v Jack [2015] CSOH 91,* in relation to the wife being taken on as a partner to an existing, pre-marital partnership:

> *"The circumstances surrounding the assumption of the defender as a partner are, on the basis of the evidence, opaque. The defender's evidence, which was unchallenged, was that she was not aware she had been made a partner in 2006 and only became aware of this fact sometime later when, having obtained part-time work in the local post office, she was surprised and queried with her employer why she was paying so much income tax. In making this enquiry she was informed it was because of the level of the income she was deriving as a partner in the business of Andrew Jack, Farmers."*

Notwithstanding occasional difficulty in establishing when a partnership commenced or when a partner joined, a more complex question is whether there has been a change to the business during the period of the marriage, and whether that change is sufficient to constitute a "new asset" acquired during the period of the marriage. There may have been an original "farm business" (whether a partnership or a sole trader) pre-dating the marriage, but the claimant may seek to argue that this business was reconstituted during the marriage, such that the current interest in the partnership is a matrimonial asset.

A further possible argument relates to Partnership Agreements. For example, if a new Partnership Agreement was signed during the marriage, was this on the basis of continuation of an existing partnership, or the constitution of a new partnership? Often, the partnership agreement will specify this, giving a "commencement date" if a new entity. An illustration of this is given in *B v B* 2011 FamLR 91. In this case, the husband was a partner in his family farming business. He had been assumed as a partner many years before the parties met (and in fact, there was evidence that he may have been as young as 14 when he became a partner). At the date of marriage, he had a 20% share in the partnership, his parents owning the other 80%. During the course of the marriage, a fresh partnership deed was executed. The partners remained the same, but the new deed reflected that the husband's parents had gifted him 15% of their respective holdings in the partnership, with the result that he now owned 50%. The wife argued that the signature of the new partnership agreement was an event which converted the husband's non-matrimonial share in the partnership to matrimonial property. Lord Woolman firmly rejected that argument. He was clear that the Deed of Partnership only affected the rights of the partners, and noted that he was unable to analyse that Deed as constituting a fresh acquisition by the husband of the 20% share he already held in the partnership, which he held both before and after that Deed of Partnership. That 20% share was accordingly not matrimonial property.

Acquisition by way of gift

Another issue which can lack clarity is whether or not a spouse's interest in a partnership has been gifted, or acquired for value. If this interest was acquired during the period of the marriage, it will be "matrimonial property" if acquired for value, but not matrimonial property if gifted. It will accordingly be necessary to consider whether there was any "consideration" for either spouse being taken on as partner; in particular, did he/she have to introduce any capital to the partnership? The intent of the spouse and the original partners (often the parents) when the spouse was taken on as a partner may also need to be considered. It will obviously be helpful if there is any contemporaneous written record of the intent to gift. If the gifter is still alive, it can also be helpful to obtain an Affidavit from them going through the transaction and their intentions – provided, of course, they are willing to put this on record.

There have been some innovative attempts to argue what can constitute "consideration" in this regard. Going back to the case of *B v B,* the wife's agents argued that the transfer to the husband during the marriage of a 30% stake in the partnership by his parents was not a gift. She argued that the "consideration" was that this transfer improved the death duty position, and so there was a benefit to the partnership, which took away the element of gift. The Court was however clear that any such improvement to the death duty did not alter the central fact that the transfer was a gift, and that the husband's parents made over their respective share of the partnership without any financial return.

In the case of *Jack v Jack [2015] CSOH 91* and *[2016] CSIH 75,* the wife similarly sought to argue that the husband's acquisition of his interest in the partnership from his father was not a gift. The father had acquired funds from sale of land, and introduced part of those funds to the farm business, by way of a loan from him to the business. The father later instructed the farm accountants to treat the amount of the loan as having been gifted to his son, and the accountants did so, treating the sum as capital introduced by the son/husband. The husband's capital account had been overdrawn prior to that gift. The wife sought to argue that the father's instructions to the accountants were insufficient to transfer the loan account to the husband, and a formal deed of assignation was required. Without this assignation, it was argued that there could not be said to be a gift of this sum. Both the Outer and Inner House rejected this argument, noting that a valid assignation was made in accordance with proper accounting practice, and the husband therefore obtained his interest in the partnership by way of gift, meaning that it was not matrimonial property which should be shared.

Increases of value within a capital account

This is a rather controversial issue, perhaps with scope for fuller debate in a future case. The first view would suggest that interest in a partnership should be treated as akin to a bank account. The partner has a right to share in the firm's profits; if that partner retains profits in the partnership capital account, one argument would be to treat those retained funds as "matrimonial property". This arises from one interpretation of *Marshall v Marshall 2007 Fam LR 48* and (to a lesser extent) *Vance v Vance 1997 SLT (Sh Ct) 71* (where the decision related only to the admissibility of averments). In *Marshall*, the husband had been a partner in a farming partnership since before the marriage. Between the date of marriage and the date of separation, there had been an increase in the balance of the husband's partnership capital account. The wife sought to have this taken into account and argued that she had made a contribution to the business by which the husband had gained an economic advantage, meaning he was able to retain some of his profit in the partnership and minimise his drawings, so increasing the balance on the capital account. Lord Hardie concluded that it was appropriate for the increase in the balance on the husband's capital account between marriage and separation to be included as matrimonial property.

The second, contrary view is to cite *Whittome v Whittome (No. 1) 1994 SLT* 114, and the well-established dicta that increases in value of non-matrimonial assets cannot themselves be a matrimonial asset. Accordingly, the argument is that any such retained profits are merely an increase in the value of the pre-existing partnership interest, and so remain non-matrimonial property. That would still allow for using any significant uplift in the capital account (or indeed other non-matrimonial property) as a benchmark for measuring and then awarding a suitable sum to the other spouse in reflection of an economic disadvantage claim (which will be covered in more detail in Chapter Ten).

CHAPTER FOUR

THE FARM BUSINESS – OTHER BUSINESS ENTITIES

<u>Sole Traders</u>

A sole trader is a business run by one individual, who is self-employed. Income tax is due on the business's profits, and the business owner is personally liable for any losses. The business may trade just under the name of the individual, or alternatively the business may use a trading name.

For the purposes of divorce, the net value of the business will be an asset in the business holder's sole name, if falling within the definition as set out in the 1985 Act, being whether the asset (i.e. the business) was acquired during the period of the marriage but before separation, with the exception of any inheritance or gift from a third party.

A sole trader business may be created or change in form during the course of the marriage, such as to create a matrimonial asset. An example of this is the recent case of *Bradbury v Bradbury 2021 CSOH 113*, where the defender husband operated a sole trader business at one farm prior to and then during the marriage; that farm was then sold, and first one and then a second new farm acquired during the marriage. The two farming businesses run by the defender as a sole trader in respect of those new farms were matrimonial property.

Issues of valuation will be considered in Chapter Nine below.

Companies

A company is a separate legal entity from the owners. The owners of the company are the shareholders, and for the purposes of divorce, the asset to be considered and potentially valued is the shareholding owned by either or both spouses, not the underlying business, although the value of the underlying business will be a highly relevant consideration in the value of the shares.

The rules for the internal governance of a company are set out in its articles of association, and occasionally also in a shareholders' agreement, the terms of which may supplement or replace the terms of the articles. Those articles, and certain other business information, including statutory accounts, can be found online at Companies House. Although Companies House can be an excellent starting point for information gathering (particularly if the client is uncertain of basic points, such as when the company was set up, or who owns what shareholding), be aware that certain relevant information is not filed there. Most farming companies will qualify as a "small company", currently defined as a company which for accounting periods beginning on or after 1 January 2016 meets at least 2 of the following conditions: annual turnover must be not more than £10.2 million; the balance sheet total must be not more than £5.1 million; the average number of employees must be not more than 50. Qualifying as a "small company" means that the members may choose to submit abridged accounts to Companies House, and also that they may elect not to file either the profit and loss accounts, or the director's report to the accounts.

Accordingly, in addition to the information publicly available on Companies House, it would be sensible to seek further documentation as follows:

- Full financial statements, rather than abridged, including a full profit and loss account;

- Monthly management accounts (if prepared);

- Any shareholders agreement.

For divorce, the central questions are whether the shareholding is "matrimonial property"; and how this should be valued. With regard to matrimonial property, the definition is set out in the 1985 Act, as noted above.

CHAPTER FIVE

THE FARMLAND

<u>What land is owned?</u>

It is possible for there to be complexities or ambiguities over exactly what farmland is owned. In fact, the legal ownership of the land might be quite different to what your client thinks it is, or how things operate on a day-to-day basis. Therefore, one of the divorce solicitor's first jobs, at an early stage, is to obtain a report on the full extent of the land owned.

This task will be considerably easier if the farmland is now in the Land Register as opposed to the General Register of Sasines, but as at the time of writing, this cannot be guaranteed. The Sasine Register is a register of individual title deeds, which may or may not contain plans of the land registered. The Sasines-registered title should contain a description of the land, which may be by reference back to an earlier deed (in which case that earlier deed will need to be consulted also) or may be particular, describing the nature and length of the boundaries. If there is a plan, that plan may be "demonstrative" (in which case the written description prevails over the plan) or "taxative" (in which case the plan prevails over the written description). Particularly if boundary features have changed over the years or decades, it may be difficult to establish what, exactly, is contained within the title. It is also possible for Sasines titles to overlap, resulting in boundary disputes. Lastly, there may be sales of small parcels of the original land, which mean that the extent of the current land needs to be pieced together from a number of different dispositions.

In contrast, the Land Register, introduced in 1981, is a map-based register, using the Ordnance Survey map. It is not possible for land registered in the Land Register to overlap. The intent is that all land in Scotland be moved from the Sasines to the Land Register, but that process has been slow, particularly in rural areas. Prior to December 2014, "first registration" in the Land Register was only triggered by sale of the land. Since that date, voluntary registration of land has been possible, and encouraged, and there is also the option for the Keeper of the Registers to initiate registration. The stated aim of the Scottish Government is for all land to be contained within the Land Register by 2024.

Who is the Landowner?

This is another seemingly obvious, yet important question, which can be more complex than it appears.

First, although your client thinks of this as "my land", title to the land might actually be held in joint names, either with the spouse, or perhaps with another family member. Secondly, if the farm business is run as a partnership, title to the land might be held by one or both spouses in their capacity as trustees for the partnership, meaning the partnership will own the land, not your client (or their spouse). If so, the disposition may record that the land has been transferred to the farmer (and others) "*as partners and trustees of the firm of Farm Partnership*". But if the disposition doesn't say this and (on the face of the document) dispones the land to one or both of the couple as individuals, be aware that the land could still be a partnership asset. This will be covered in more detail in Chapter 6.

If the spouse does not own the land, but is instead a tenant of the farmland, consider whether there is any value in the tenancy to be taken into account as a matrimonial asset. This will depend on the type of tenancy and security of tenure.

Who occupies the land?

It is also important to establish who occupies the land, as distinct from ownership, given that this may impact on the value of the land and when and how it can be sold. There may be third party occupiers, such as agricultural/residential tenants or employees living in property tied to their employment. Occasionally you may have a "grace and favour" arrangement, with an older generation or former farm worker occupying a farm cottage. That arrangement could also be formalised into a legal binding situation, such as an older generation of the family having a "liferent" over the property. Note that a liferent interest may be recorded in the title, or may be contained in a separate Deed.

What restrictions are there about use of the land?

Restrictions on use of land might be imposed by the planning system. Any planning permissions which have been granted will need to be checked. For example, a restriction on the use of properties built on the farmland – such as that erection of any new property on the land is conditional upon it being occupied by an agricultural employee and his/her immediate family – could be set out in a planning condition or (either in addition or by way of alternative) may be set out in a planning obligation in terms of Section 75 of the Town and Country Planning (Scotland) Act 1997.

A planning permission – and the conditions to which it is subject – continues to apply despite a change in ownership, as the benefit of planning permission 'runs with the land'. It may be necessary to check if the planning permission and its conditions have been complied with. This will involve a physical check of development which has taken place, considered against the terms of the planning permission. It may involve checking that no development has taken place without any necessary planning permissions having been obtained.

A breach of planning control can result in enforcement action being taken by the local authority. There are detailed rules regarding when enforcement action can no longer be taken after the passage of time, with the time limits generally depending on whether the breach involves physical development undertaken without planning permission, breach of a planning condition, or an unauthorised change of use. If there is doubt, an application can be made to the local authority for a certificate to confirm that development which has taken place is lawful.

If a planning obligation under section 75 has been entered into, this will usually be registered in either the Sasines or Land Register; if registered, this obligation will again run with the land and bind successive owners.

In either scenario, it is possible that in the intervening period, the planning situation in that area may have changed, meaning that an application to remove the planning condition or to vary or discharge the planning obligation may be successful. Clearly, both of these can have a significant impact on value, as well as restricting options for occupation or use of the property (and so options for settlement).

In addition to planning restrictions, the title to the land might also contain title restrictions which restrict or regulate the use to which the land can be put, although this has become less prevalent following feudal reform.

<u>Is there a security over the land?</u>

There may be bank borrowing secured over the farmland. Again, it is important to establish whose name the borrowing is in (the farmer as an individual; the married couple; the partnership; or some other combination), as well as what area of land (if any) the borrowing is secured against, particularly if sections of farmland have been bought and sold over the years.

Where land is in a company, the security may take the form of a floating charge.

Sometimes security is granted to secure an obligation *ad factum praestandum* (to do a specific act). An example of this would be in the context of an option agreement, where the developer contracts for an option (subject to obtaining necessary planning and other consents) to buy or lease land from the landowner, and the security is used to secure the landowner's obligations in respect of that option.

Is the land matrimonial property?

The main question for the family lawyer (and the client) is obviously whether or not the farmland falls within the definition of "matrimonial property". Going back to the definition of matrimonial property per the 1985 Act, the exclusions are if the land was acquired pre-marriage, or was inherited, or was a gift from third parties. It will usually be fairly clear if land was acquired pre-marriage or has been inherited, but it can be a bit more complex to prove that land has been gifted for no consideration.

Was the land gifted?

Issues to consider are:

- Does the disposition recount that the transfer was for *"love favour and affection"* rather than for consideration?

- Was stamp duty paid? If exempt from stamp duty, under which category?

- Is there any record of the intention to gift, whether in the disposition itself or elsewhere?

- Are the spouse and the transferor (if still alive) both clear that that the intention was for this to be a gift? Would they be prepared to set this out in an affidavit?

- Has there been any consideration of any type? Bear in mind this can happen in various ways:

    o *A land swap or "contract of excambion":* It is not uncommon for land to be exchanged within farming families. If such an exchange happens during marriage, then the land acquired by the farmer or spouse will have been acquired for value in the course of that transaction – even if the original piece of land was acquired by way of gift or inheritance.

    o *A side agreement:* Another possible scenario is for land to be gifted by the farmer's parents, but for there to be an agreement or understanding that the parents remain in one of the houses on the farmland, or for the parents to be paid a monthly amount by way of "pension". If there is such an arrangement, does it amount to "consideration" so that the land was not actually gifted? If the transferors are staying in a farmhouse which is no longer owned by them, are they doing so for free, or are they paying independently assessed market rent, or somewhere in between? Is there any written agreement documenting this? Is it evident from the farm accounts or the spouses' bank accounts that money has gone from a spouse to the transferors, whether in one lump sum or regularly? If so, are those transfers actually consideration/payment for the transfer of land, even if not officially recorded as such?

- *Payment at undervalue:* What if £50,000 was paid for land worth £500,000? To the author's knowledge, this is not yet an issue which has been dealt with comprehensively in terms of the case law. On the one hand, it might be argued that this was not "full" consideration for the asset, and so would not all fall within the definition of matrimonial property. On the other hand, the argument could run that inadequate or not, consideration was made, and so the land would fall within the definition of matrimonial property, but (importantly) would be subject to a source of funds argument (see Chapter Ten). This argument was canvassed in *MacLean v MacLean 2001 FamLR 118,* where the wife argued that a land acquisition should be treated as a gift, on the basis that land which she had purchased for £60,000 from her mother was actually worth £200,000 with vacant possession. The Court held in that case that factually, the land was probably worth around £80,000 and so *"the price paid by the pursuer ... is not so far out of line with the open market value ... as to indicate that the transaction was a gift".* (para 21-16). That would seem to indicate that, despite that factual finding, the Court did not reject the argument out of hand; and so it might be possible to have a price which was sufficiently out of line with market value as to indicate at least an element of gift.

What about a house built on non-matrimonial land?

This is the issue which was considered in the interesting Sheriff Appeal case of *Grant v. Grant [2018] SAC (Civ) 4*. In terms of the facts, there was a plot of land owned by the husband before the marriage, before he and his wife were in any established relationship. During the course of their relationship, the couple then built a kit house upon the land. The Sheriff at first instance decided that the land on which the house had been built was not matrimonial property, whereas the building materials that came to represent the physical embodiment of the house were matrimonial property. Both parties appealed. The husband relied upon principles of property law – he contended that the land was not matrimonial property, and as the house acceded to and became part of that land, the house was also not matrimonial property.

The Sheriff Principal disagreed with both the husband and the Sheriff, and determined that the house, and the land upon which it was erected, was a single item of property, not two separate ones. However, the Sheriff Principal then went on to say that this single item of property can only have been "acquired" *as and when then house was completed.* He held that the law of accession which the husband was seeking to rely upon only regulates property ownership and did not affect the issue of whether or not a particular asset is "matrimonial property" for the purpose of the 1985 Act. The Sheriff Principal did however finish with the caveat that "*the identification of matrimonial property is but one step in determining what orders for financial provision should be made. The 1985 Act gives to the Sheriff certain discretionary powers to ensure a division is equitable to both parties*".

As a minimum, the decision reached by the Court in *Grant* is not particularly intuitive. Would a farming couple truly appreciate that the act of building a house would change the character of the land from non-matrimonial to matrimonial? It also seems a decision which is likely to give rise to considerable difficulties for farming cases in particular, and so may be a point of future litigation. If the Sheriff Principal's decision was upheld in future litigation, there remains a question as to how far this doctrine goes? For example, if a building and garden ground was built on farmland extending to many acres of land, would it only be the house and perhaps a small area of adjoining garden ground which could conceivably be converted to "matrimonial property" – and not the entire acreage of farmland? Or what about the situation where there was a building on non-matrimonial property, but one entirely unsuitable for habitation – for example, if there was a shed or old barn, to which extensive work was done to make it into a family home? Would that also "convert" the land on which the building stands to matrimonial property?

CHAPTER SIX

IS THE FARMLAND WITHIN THE PARTNERSHIP?

As noted in Chapter Five, the question of whether or not land is owned by one or more individuals in their personal capacity, or in their name but on behalf of the partnership, can be a tricky one. It is also a question which can make a very significant difference to the matrimonial pot.

If the land would otherwise be non-matrimonial property, but part or all of the interest in the partnership is matrimonial, it can be in the claimant's interest to argue that the land is held by the partnership.

This can however work the other way round. If the partnership interest is not matrimonial property, then it can be in the claimant's interest to argue that the land is held outwith the partnership.

To ascertain this, we need to get to grips with partnership law, starting with sections 20 to 22 of the Partnership Act 1890.

Land bought with partnership funds

Perhaps the simplest question is whether or not the land has been acquired with partnership funds. If so, the Partnership Act sets out a statutory presumption that such land is a partnership asset.

Section 21:

> "*Unless the contrary intention appears, property bought with money belonging to the firm is deemed to have been bought on account of the firm*".

It is however possible to argue that the statutory presumption has been displaced, and that was what was attempted in *Marshall v Marshall 2007 Fam LR 48*. In that case, the husband had been a partner in a farming partnership with his brother and mother for more than a decade prior to marriage. During the course of the marriage, the partnership had sold the farmland that it had originally farmed, and had bought two new pieces of land. Those pieces of land were bought using partnership funds, but title to them was taken in the names of the two brothers as individuals and not, on the face of the title deeds, as trustees and partners of the farming partnership.

It was argued on behalf of the wife that there should be no enquiry into the issue of beneficial ownership. Instead, the position put forward was that the title deeds were probative documents and they disclosed that the husband and his brother owned the land between them in equal shares, as individuals. The husband however asserted that despite the wording of the dispositions, the land was truly a partnership asset. It had been bought with partnership funds. The family regarded it as partnership property. They did not understand why title had been taken in the names of the brothers – this was a matter they left to the lawyers. The farm accountants did not include the land in the partnership accounts, but explained that the reason for them having not done so was that the previous accountants had followed that practice and they (the new accountants) felt they could not depart from it. However, a summary of partnership assets produced for the benefit of the bank prior to separation, included reference to the land as a partnership asset. In this case, the Court was persuaded that it was appropriate to look behind the title deeds; taking into account section 21 of Partnership Act, the land was partnership property, was not matrimonial property, and so was out of the reckoning.

A further case involving an unsuccessful attempt to rebut the section 21 presumption is *Longmuir v Moffat [2009] CSIH 19*. That case involved an executry dispute, rather than divorce, but centred around the same issues, being again a situation where title to the land was taken in the sole name of one of the partners. The land was purchased using a cheque drawn on the partnership bank account. One party sought to argue that the presumption had been rebutted, due to the fact that title was taken in the deceased individual's sole name; a standard security was granted with no reference to, or acknowledgement of, the partnership having any interest in the land; and the individual on the title lodged tax returns which treated the land as his personal asset. The Court first noted that *"a recorded title such as that held to Merchanthall Farm by the appellant, while being conclusive as to real right, was not conclusive as regards beneficial ownership ... There are numerous cases in which the court has been prepared to examine the issue of beneficial ownership in the face of a contention that the title to heritable property did not reflect the true position regarding such ownership"*. On the matter of section 21, the Court noted the evidence in support of rebuttal, but also evidence in support of the presumption, in particular the inclusion of the land in the balance sheet of the partnership accounts. The Court accordingly upheld a previous decision of the arbiter that the section 21 presumption was not rebutted in this case.

Land acquired for the purposes of partnership business

This can be a rather more complex scenario to disentangle. In terms of section 20(1):

> *"All property and rights and interests in property originally brought into the partnership stock or acquired, whether by*

purchase or otherwise, on account of the firm, or for the purposes and in the course of the partnership business, are called in this Act partnership property, and must be held and applied by the partners exclusively for the purposes of the partnership and in accordance with the partnership agreement."

This section accordingly applies to land not bought with partnership funds, but which has been acquired *"on account of the firm, or for the purposes and in the course of the partnership business"*, rather than just being held separately by an individual or individuals.

One of the best illustrations of how to consider this issue is the case of *Jack v Jack [2016] CSIH 75*, a case which went to Inner House on issue of treatment of land, and whether this was included as an asset of the farm partnership or not. In *Jack,* the land had been transferred by the husband's father to husband, at the time the husband had set up the farming partnership. The Inner House noted that there were various different ways in which the land could have been dealt with. The husband's father could have expressly declared that the land was partnership property; he could have granted a lease of the land in favour of the partnership, in which case rent would likely have been payable and the terms of the lease specified; he could have granted an express right of occupation in favour of the partnership in the form of a licence; or he could have just allowed the partnership to occupy the land on an informal basis.

The Court observed that this last option was a very common arrangement in practice, where land or premises belonging to an individual are made available to a partnership in which that person or members of the family are partners. There are a number of advantageous reasons, including tax reasons, why this arrangement is often used, including that the property cannot be used to satisfy the rights of the partnership's creditors.

The Court was clear that this last option was the arrangement which had been set up by the Pursuer husband's father. They gave several reasons why they came to this conclusion. First, the Dispositions granted in favour of the Pursuer were granted in absolute terms to him, rather than being subject to any trust rights in favour of the partnership. The Court noted that it had it been intended that the land should have been partnership property, it would have been very straightforward to make an express provision to that effect, either in the Disposition or in a separate Trust Deed, but this was not done. Secondly, the Court noted that the land was not included as an asset in the balance sheet of the partnership. The Court noted that if it had been intended that the land should be partnership property, it should have been included in as an asset, and the fact that it was not was in their opinion *"a strong indication"* there was no intention that the land should be partnership property. Lastly, no evidence was led of any intention to make the husband's interest in the land partnership property at any time since the disposition.

Among the failed arguments put forward by the wife was the fact the farm had been occupied by the partnership and the partnership paid the outgoings on the land. The Inner House gave this argument somewhat short shrift, noting (at para 25):

> *"In our view these factors are of little significance. If a partnership is given a licence to occupy, the purpose is clearly that it should use the land in question; thus the fact of use is neutral as between ownership and a mere licence. Furthermore, in a number of cases it has been clearly held that the mere use of heritable property for the purposes of a partnership is not sufficient to stamp the property with the character of partnership property: Miller, Partnership, page 393. In our opinion, there are good reasons for this: it permits a proprietor of land to make it available to a partnership without its becoming partnership property, which can have the advantages described at paragraph*

[18] above. So far as outgoings are concerned, if an informal licence to occupy is granted, it is normal for the occupier to pay the outgoings on the land; that is only fair, as the occupier otherwise receives a gratuitous benefit. Consequently we do not regard this factor as of importance."

Useful English cases on partnership land

Although clearly not binding on the Scottish court, English farming cases can provide a useful point of comparison, in areas where the law is the same or similar. Differences in land law, contracts and the fact that English partnerships do not have a separate legal personality will all need to be borne in mind, but the following English cases may nevertheless be of some interest to Scottish practitioners.

The case of *Ham v Bell and others [2016] EWHC 1791 (Ch)* involved a farming partnership dispute between parents and their son. The parents had farmed in partnership with each other for many years; they then decided to form a new partnership with the son. The question was whether the farmland (which had been an asset of the old partnership) became an asset of the new partnership. The land had been included in the partnership accounts of the new partnership for the first four years; new accountants then took over, and (at the parents' request) the land was left out of the accounts going forward. The judgment in one respect is very similar to the outcome of *Jack v Jack*, in its emphasis that it is not necessary for farmland to be a farm partnership asset; and that use of this land by the partnership, or the fact that the partnership paid for improvements, did not make it so. A difference from *Jack* is that in *Ham v Bell*, there was no separate gift of the land to the son – it had been an asset of the previous partnership, and the question was who owned it now? The Court held that there had been no discussion between the parties about whether the land would be an asset of the new partnership; that if accounts do not reflect what was agreed, they fall to be disregarded; and that the first few years' of accounts were prepared on a mistaken basis, simply carrying on the accounting treatment which had applied to the old farm partnership, which mistake was then corrected. The land therefore belonged to the parents, not the partnership.

In *Wild v Wild [2018] 2197 (Ch)*, there were proceedings for dissolution of the farm partnership resulting from an acrimonious sibling fall-out. The claimant (one of the siblings) in that case argued that the main farm and farmhouse were partnership assets, to be taken into account in the winding-up; the defendants (the mother, the other brother and the brother's wife) claimed otherwise. In this case, the land had been held by the (now deceased) father, and was passed to the mother following his death. The Court determined that a reference to "property" in the earliest accounts available was a reference to the farmland, but held (para 49) that *"[T]he inclusion of an asset in partnership accounts as partnership property is evidence that it is partnership property and is likely to be very powerful and persuasive evidence but it is not conclusive of that question."* The Court also noted that as a matter of principle, one partner cannot unilaterally cause his or her property to become a partnership asset without either the prior agreement or subsequent ratification of the other partners (para 35). In this case, the land could only have become partnership property at the commencement of the partnership between the parents and the First Defendant son (then aged 16). The Court held that had not happened, given that it was extremely unlikely in the particular family circumstances that the father would have ceded control of his land asset in that way; and that the father had instead included the land in the accounts, without discussion or agreement with his son, and possibly without thought as to the potential implications.

The two cases together therefore sound something of a note of caution about reliance on accounts alone in determining whether land is indeed a partnership asset, where the other evidence points to the alternative.

CHAPTER SEVEN

INTERACTION OF MATRIMONIAL AND PARTNERSHIP LAW

One of the difficulties for matrimonial lawyers in dealing with farming cases is knowing what can happen in the context of the divorce, and what needs to happen in the context of separate partnership litigation (in the absence of agreement). Getting this wrong can cause considerable problems.

Orders for transfer of an interest in a partnership

The first, and perhaps obvious, issue to point out is that it is competent to seek transfer of an interest in a partnership in the context of divorce proceedings. Section 8 of the 1985 Act states:

> *(1) In an action for divorce, either party to the marriage and in an action for dissolution of a civil partnership, either partner may apply to the court for one or more of the following orders—*
>
> *… (aa) an order for the transfer of property to him by the other party to the action…"*

"Property" in terms of s8(1)(aa) includes an interest in a partnership, and such transfer has been sought and granted in a variety of cases (e.g. *Jack v Jack* [2015] CSOH 91; *Parker v Parker* [2014] CSOH 159; *M v M* 2014 Fam LR 116).

Sale or transfer of a partnership asset

In contrast to transfer of an entire interest in a partnership, what is not competent in the context of matrimonial proceedings is sale or transfer of one particular partnership asset, at least without the consent (express or inferred) of all partners.

This is set out in the decision in *Clarke v Clarke 2007 SLT (Sh Ct) 54* and *2007 SLT (Sh Ct) 86*. Mr and Mrs Clarke were partners in a farm business. In that case, the Court had to consider craves for sale of various partnership assets, the milk quota, and Single Farm Payment, all described as *"owned by the parties' firm of Auchlea Farm"*. The Sheriff Principal upheld the decision of the Sheriff that an incidental order for sale of these assets was not competent, noting that these were all assets to which s 20(1) of the Partnership Act 1890 applied. Accordingly, they must be *"held and applied by the partners exclusively for the purposes of the partnership, and in accordance with the partnership agreement"* in terms of that section. Without any consent to amend the partnership agreement so as to allow the same, the Sheriff Principal held that, if the Sheriff were to grant orders in terms of these two craves in pursuance of s 14(2)(a), *"he would be cutting across the provisions of the parties' contract and this in my opinion he could not competently do in the face of s 20(1) of the 1890 Act"*.

However, a rather different decision was made in the same case about sale of the partnership land. In this case, as was apparently clear from the face of the disposition, the land was held on behalf of the partnership. However, the Initial Writ sought sale and division of *"**the parties' heritable property**"* (emphasis added). At first instance, there was no alternative view put forward by the defender – that the heritable property was actually owned by the partnership, not the parties – and no plea-in-law as to the competency of the relevant craves. The case then proceeded as undefended, and an interlocutor was granted for sale of *"the parties' heritable property"* and subsequent division of the proceeds. Some three months later, the defender then sought recall of this interlocutor, on the basis that the farmland was actually partnership property.

This did not however succeed, with the Sheriff Principal holding that the incidental order for sale was competent. He referred to section 19 of the Partnership Act 1890, which provides: *"The mutual rights and duties of partners, whether ascertained by agreement or defined by this Act, may be varied by the consent of all the partners, and such consent may be either express or inferred from a course of dealing."* The Sheriff noted that he could understand why the incidental order would have been incompetent if there had been other partners in the firm separate to the divorce proceedings and these partners had not consented to the sale; and also that the order would have been incompetent if the defender himself had opposed it. However, in the circumstances of the case, he found the *"irresistible inference"* was that the defender had consented to the sale of the farm in terms of the pursuer's craves, and had therefore consented to a variation of the partnership to accommodate this, meaning that the interlocutor for sale was perfectly competent and *"does not cease to be a competent order simply because, for whatever reason, the defender has now changed his mind and regrets having given his consent."* The case is therefore a helpful explanation of the interaction between the competency of the Court for orders on divorce and the Partnership Act 1890; but also a rather salutary lesson about the need to think clearly, preferably at an early stage, about what is and isn't a partnership asset.

Preventing dissolution

A further issue which may arise is if one party wishes to continue with the partnership, and the other wishes it to cease. This was the situation in *Robertson v Robertson 2009 Fam LR 13*, where the wife sought an interim interdict preventing the husband from dissolving, whether by notice of dissolution or otherwise, their limited partnership. The interim interdict was sought in terms of section 18 of the Family Law (Scotland) Act 1985, in terms of which the party claiming financial provision may seek to interdict the other party from effecting any transfer or transaction involving property which is likely to have the effect of defeating in whole or in part their financial claim.

In *Robertson,* the interim interdict was granted at first instance by the Sheriff, but overturned on appeal to the Sheriff Principal. The Sheriff Principal noted that the mischief which section 18 was designed to combat was the giving away of money or property to the prejudice of the claimant and held as follows: *"In my opinion the giving of a notice of dissolution of a partnership is not in this context a transaction involving property. It is merely a notice indicating that one party to a contract of partnership proposes to give six months' notice of dissolution of the partnership. It is something the defender and respondent is entitled to do in terms of the partnership agreement. I do not believe it was the intention of the legislation to prevent partners withdrawing from a business relationship which they did not wish to continue."*

The business sense of the judgment is clear; but it perhaps remains to be seen whether a higher court may take a wider interpretation of the meaning of "transaction" involving property in terms of section 18, particularly if the prejudice to the claimant of the partnership coming to an end was stark.

Varying the terms of a partnership agreement

If dissolution of a partnership cannot be prevented in terms of the 1985 Act, can the partnership terms nevertheless be varied in the context of divorce proceedings? *Clarke v Clarke* (above) sets out the possibility of doing so by consent, in terms of section 19 of the Partnership Act 1890. However, if that consent is not forthcoming, the answer would seem to be that it is not possible to vary the terms, on the basis of the short yet clear decision in *Robertson v Robertson 2003 SLT 208*. In that case, the pursuer husband sought to utilise Section 14(2)(h) of the 1985 Act, which allows for the making of an incidental order in a divorce action *"setting aside or varying any term of an antenuptial or postnuptial marriage settlement"*. He argued that the farm partnership agreement fell within that definition, and so sought variation of a clause relating to valuation of a retiring or deceased partner's share. The Court gave this somewhat short shrift, holding that the partnership agreement was not a marriage settlement, however wide an interpretation was given to this statutory term, but a business arrangement, independent of marital status. As such, the parties had to abide by their bargain, and no variation was granted.

CHAPTER EIGHT

OTHER FARMING ASSETS AND DIVERSIFICATION

There are a number of unique assets to farm businesses, as well as farms who have sought to diversify in a number of ways. This chapter is a brief overview of the more specialist assets or issues which may appear in a farming divorce case.

Subsidies

The Basic Payment Scheme in Scotland allows farmers to apply for entitlements based on the land they farm and activity they undertake. It replaces the previous Single Farm Payments Scheme. A farmer can participate in the Scheme under a number of conditions, including if that farmer:

- is an "Active Farmer" who is involved in acceptable agricultural activity;

- farms a minimum of three hectares of eligible land;

- holds Basic Payment Scheme entitlements, either through an original award or having acquired them by transfer;

- submits a claim in the form of a Single Application Form (IACS) aid application (the deadline for which is 15 May each year, after which late submission will result in deductions); and

- meets a number of conditions for maintenance of the land, including environmentally-friendly practices ("greening").

The IACS application is made annually, with payments being made throughout that year. Additional payments are available for those who fall within the definition of the "Young Farmer" scheme.

Basic Payment Scheme entitlements can be transferred, either by sale or by lease, either together with land or separately. They can however only be transferred to someone who similarly falls within the required definition of "active farmer" involved in agricultural activity.

For the purposes of divorce, the important point to note is that the entitlements in terms of the Basic Payment Scheme have a value. This asset is not usually included in annual accounts for the business, and so will need to be considered, valued and (if appropriate) added to any accounts to be prepared for the purposes of divorce.

Renewable energy

This has been an area of diversification for Scottish farmers for some time, in particular on-shore wind turbines and run-of-river hydro schemes (taking advantage of the Scottish weather). Although the previous "Feed-in Tariff" (which allowed sale of excess energy to the national grid) closed to new applicants in early 2019, the Scottish Government focus on renewable energy may result in alternative incentives or schemes being put in place, given that the stated policy is to increase the number of commercial onshore turbines from about 6000 to 10,000 by 2030.

The planning and construction costs of such schemes are high, and it is therefore usual for the risk and cost to be taken on by a developer, with the site leased from the farmer for a set period. For the purposes of divorce, this site and lease has a value. The landlord of the lease will need to be ascertained (whether the farm partnership, or a separate business, or the farmer or couple as individuals) and appropriate account taken of the value. If appropriate in terms of ownership, the land valuer may be able to cover this in any valuation of the farmland. Details of the site and the lease will need to be made available to the valuer. There may alternatively be an option to take a lease, perhaps dependent on future planning permission, in which case this is likely to be secured by an *ad factum praestandum* security – the option itself may well affect land value.

Radio masts

Similarly to renewable developments, there may be a mast site on the land, usually subject to a fairly long lease. That will again have a value, to be taken into account in any valuation of the farmland.

Planning and development

Considerable value can attach to land because of its development potential, for example for housing or renewable energy development. As the value per hectare for a residential development site will usually far outstrip the best agricultural land values, this may well merit investigation. A key issue here can be whether such development is supported by the local authority's policies. Landowners will often adopt a long-term strategy towards ensuring that appropriate allocations are secured for their land in the local authority's Local Development Plan, thereby enhancing development opportunities and therefore value.

Any such development potential should be investigated, to take into account in terms of the "hope value" for the land. This hope value is unlikely to be accounted for in the figure for the land in any business accounts. It is a matter for a land valuer, and will very much depend on what stage the development is at – whether there any verbal or written agreement (including an option agreement) in place between a potential developer and the farmer; whether the proposed development is supported by planning policy; whether planning permission has been granted; and if any appeal stages for planning permission or any legal challenges to the grant of planning permissions have run their course. This will also depend upon when the valuation is to be carried out – whether retrospectively at "relevant date" (in which case the timing of all of the above as at that date is the key factor), or at current date.

Future land developments can be extremely valuable, and so should not be lost sight of in a divorce case, where the focus may be on the current value of the land purely for agricultural purposes. Having said that, if the development is not guaranteed to go ahead, it is obviously a rather conditional value. It can therefore be helpful to consider some innovative solutions for a fair outcome, where a future windfall is a possibility, rather than one person taking all of the risk as well as all of the potential benefit. One option might be to keep or put an area of land in joint names, particularly if this relates to a small potential site or wayleave, so that both parties can share equally in any development if this does come good. Another option would be an agreement that although the development land remains in one spouse's sole name, the other spouse benefits from either a fixed sum or a percentage of the uplift in value on the land if a potential development comes good. Clearly, any such agreement would need to be carefully thought through.

Wayleave

It is possible for land value to be enhanced by wayleaves across the land, e.g. to turbines or mast sites, and this is again something to be aware of in relation to future planning and development, per the above.

Holiday lets

In some farms, diversification has taken the form of renovation of existing buildings or creation of new buildings for the purpose of holiday lets or B&B – and this may increase following the travel restrictions and increase in "staycations" of 2020/21. One question is whether this is run as an entirely separate business, or as part of the main farm business. If separate, does that business own the land on which the holiday let is situated or not?

Lease of equipment

Does the client lease out, or carry on a contracting business using, some of the (expensive) farm equipment? If so, again, is this run as a separate business, or as part of the main farm business?

Natural capital

Natural capital is set to become an ever more important concept in future, in essence seeking to assign a capital value to elements of nature which are of general benefit to the public. In farming, this can include native tree-planting, re-wilding, creating wildflower corridors between farms, peat restoration and biodiversity. Increasingly, these initiatives can add value and so should be taken into account.

Forests and fishing

A further standard question should be whether there is any woodland to be valued (which can have considerable value if there is standing timber ready to be felled). It should also be noted that fishing and other sporting rights might be held separate to ownership of the land, and so have a separate value.

CHAPTER NINE

GETTING VALUATIONS AND EXPERT ADVICE

There are generally a number of different valuations to obtain and coordinate in a farming divorce, some of which are common to other business valuations on divorce, and some of which are more unique. This chapter will cover general issues common to all valuations, as well as the specific valuers likely to be involved and the issues to consider for each.

<u>General issues for valuations</u>

There has been helpful guidance given over recent years regarding expert witnesses both generally, and in divorce cases in particular. A good place to start is the Supreme Court case of *Kennedy v Cordia (Services) [2016] UKSC 6*. Para 44 sets out four considerations which the Court considered governed the admissibility of skilled evidence: (i) whether the proposed skilled evidence will assist the court in its task; (ii) whether the witness has the necessary knowledge and experience; (iii) whether the witness is impartial in his or her presentation and assessment of the evidence; and (iv) whether there is a reliable body of knowledge or experience to underpin the expert's evidence.

Of these requirements, impartiality (or the lack thereof) is an area that can cause particular problems. On that aspect, the Court in *Kennedy* re-affirmed the summary given by Cresswell J at pp 81-82 of the English case of *The Ikarian Reefer [1003] 2 Lloyd's Rep 68*, which the Court noted should be applied in Scottish civil cases and which is worth repeating in full:

"The duties and responsibilities of expert witnesses in civil cases include the following:

1. Expert evidence presented to the court should be, and should be seen to be, the independent product of the expert uninfluenced as to form or content by the exigencies of litigation.

2. An expert witness should provide independent assistance to the court by way of objective unbiased opinion in relation to matters within his expertise. An expert witness in the High Court should never assume the role of an advocate.

3. An expert witness should state the facts or assumption on which his opinion is based. He should not omit to consider material facts which could detract from his concluded opinion.

4. An expert witness should make it clear when a particular question or issue falls outside his expertise.

5. If an expert's opinion is not properly researched because he considers that insufficient data is available, then this must be stated with an indication that the opinion is no more than a provisional one. In cases where an expert witness who has prepared a report could not assert that the report contained the truth, the whole truth and nothing but the truth without some qualification, that qualification should be stated in the report.

6. If, after exchange of reports, an expert witness changes his view on a material matter having read the other side's expert's report or for any other reason, such change of view should be communicated (through legal representatives) to the other side without delay and when appropriate to the court.

7. Where expert evidence refers to photographs, plans, calculations, analyses, measurements, survey reports or other similar documents, these must be provided to the opposite party at the same time as the exchange of reports."

A recent example of consideration of expert valuers in a divorce case is found in *SCA v MMA [2020] CSOH 54*. The parties in that case operated a number of restaurants, being owned through various business vehicles, including a holding company, as a sole trader, and in partnership. Both spouses instructed commercial surveyors to value the various businesses, then asked forensic accountants to value the business entities using the information provided by the surveyors. For a number of reasons, Lady Wise concluded that she could not rely on the evidence of the surveyor instructed for the husband. First, the terms on which he had accepted his appointment and the narrative in his report did not conform to RICS standards for providing independent expert evidence. Secondly, the surveyor was potentially dealing on the husband's behalf with an ongoing valuation for the bank, at the same time as acting as an expert. The surveyor then sought to depart from his earlier view as to valuation, mid-proof and after the pursuer had closed her case, following communication with the husband. Lady Wise held that given his *"change of heart on valuation, the backdrop of the absence in his report to his duties to the court and the other errors mentioned take on more significance than they might have otherwise. ... I consider that he has allowed himself to be influenced by MMA's views on the matter. As a result he departed from the necessary position of impartiality of a witness giving opinion evidence and appeared to promote the defender's cause on valuation."*

Lastly, it is helpful to bear in mind the dicta from *Kennedy v Cordia* (at para 57) that it falls to counsel and solicitors in the first instance to assess whether a proposed witness has the necessary expertise; whether that person's evidence is admissible; and that the witness is aware of the duties imposed by the Court on an expert witness.

The date of valuation

The family lawyer should consider what date of valuation is to be used. In terms of section 10(2) of the 1985 Act, the property shall be valued at the relevant date, usually meaning the date the parties ceased to cohabit. However, for property which is to be transferred in terms of section 8(1)(aa) of the Act (being an order for the transfer of property from one spouse to the other), the "appropriate valuation date" should instead be used. Section 10(3A) of the Act defines that as the date that the parties agree, failing which the date of the making of the order for transfer of property. In exceptional circumstances, the Court can decide to use another date, although that will likely be near to the date of the making of the order for transfer.

The date of valuation will therefore depend to a significant extent on what is to happen to the property. If there are partnership or company interests, then it is likely that both current and relevant date valuations may be needed. For example, if a share in the business is to be transferred from one spouse to another, current date valuation will be needed; if another share in the business is to be retained by one of spouses, valuation as at relevant date will be needed. In relation to land, the valuation may need to be at relevant date, or current date, or both, depending on whether the land is held directly by one or more of the spouses or via a partnership, and depending on whether sale or transfer of the land (or dissolution of the partnership or transfer of partnership interests) are likely.

The land valuer

The most valuable asset in many farming cases will be the land – but whether or not this should be valued will first depends upon whether it is a matrimonial asset. As set out in detail in Chapters 5 and 6, this can often be a complex question.

Unless there has been a recent acquisition or revaluation based on current market value, it is unlikely that the value per the accounts will be a true valuation of the land, and so, in the absence of agreement, a valuation of the land for divorce purposes will usually be required. The valuer should prepare this in accordance with the guidance set out in the RICS work "Global Standards", often referred to as "The Red Book".

The issue of valuation can again often be complex, given the need to take into account a range of factors. Again, these are set out in more detail in Chapters 5 and 8, but include: accurately determining the extent of the land, any boundary disputes, and any possible issues with first registration in the Land Register; any issues caused by other occupants of the land; any restrictions on use arising from the title deeds or planning conditions/obligations; ownership or leases of wind farms and masts; and (importantly) future development potential.

The stock, subsidy and machinery valuers

The valuation per the accounts of stock and machinery may again be unsuitable for divorce purposes, with a fresh valuation required as at either relevant or current date. If at relevant date, it can be helpful for the valuer to attend the farm as close to that date as possible, as whilst a retrospective valuation can be attempted using stock and herd numbers, clearly the age and condition of the particular livestock on the farm can vary considerably over the intervening months and years.

For machinery valuations in particular, the parties and lawyers should identify beforehand, as clearly as possible, what it to be valued and what is and isn't matrimonial or partnership property. For example, there may be a number of tractors on the premises, one of which is matrimonial, but others which belong to a non-matrimonial business, or perhaps to other family members. The valuer should also clearly identify what has been valued in the report, so that there is no subsequent dispute or mix-up between assets with similar descriptions.

As noted in Chapter Eight, the family lawyer should not forget or omit entitlements and subsidies. Potential valuers would include brokers (who deal with the trade in entitlements) or local auction marts. Given the tightening of conditions in who can hold entitlements from the previous system, the value is not currently likely to be a high multiple of the annual sum.

The local auction mart may be able to provide a suitable valuer for stock, or alternatively the farmer or claimant may have good local knowledge as to whose expertise they would recommend and accept. However, the family lawyer should consider the issue of impartiality, particularly in a small rural community where the parties and prospective valuers may know each other well, or have various business and personal links. It may be safer to seek expert input from outwith the local area, in order to ensure there is no perception (whether founded or not) of partiality.

The accountants

In farming cases, the farmer will often wish to heavily involve the farm or partnership accountant, and rely only on that person's assessment or valuation. However, the farm accountant is unlikely to have the impartiality required by the Court as an expert witness, particularly where the accountant may well have an ongoing business relationship with one of the spouses but not the other. Instead, in any case proceeding to Court, an independent forensic accountant should be instructed to coordinate the land and other valuations, and provide a valuation for the farm business accordingly. This may require some difficult conversations with both the client and the adviser to explain why an independent person is needed, and that this is not somehow a criticism of the original adviser's previous work.

That is not to say that the farm accountant has no role – that person is likely to be an essential source of information, as they will usually know a considerable amount about the background and history of the farm business, and will sometimes be able to provide more of the business and legal details than the spouses themselves. Indeed, the evidence of the farm accountant has been central to some reported cases. In any case proceeding to Court, the farm accountant should work in tandem with an independent forensic accountant to provide the documentation and detail for an independent report.

The tax expert

Tax is clearly an essential area in respect of which the farming client will need advice, not from the family law solicitor, but from a tax expert. The role of the family law solicitor is to signpost the client to the need to get expert advice on this, rather than know all of the ins and outs of the tax legislation themselves. It can however be helpful for the family lawyer to have a broad overview, so that this signposting can be done.

The main issue to highlight is Capital Gains Tax ("CGT"). CGT may be incurred on sale or transfer of land, or on transfer of an interest in a farm partnership, or transfer of a shareholding in a farm company. Tax experts can advise on the possibility of any exemptions, as well as the detailed rules relating to transfers between spouses in the tax year of separation. Urgent advice may be needed as to the timing of any of transfers, given the rules allowing transfers on a "no gain, no loss" basis between spouses during the tax year of separation. It is clearly best to consider this at leisure, well in advance of the tax year end, rather than at the start of April. See Chapter Twelve for consideration of this in the context of transfer of an interest in a partnership.

CHAPTER TEN

ARGUING UNEQUAL DIVISION

Special circumstances

Given the frequency in which farming assets stem from a gifted, inherited or pre-marriage source, "source of funds" is a common argument for the farmer spouse. If it cannot successfully be argued that the farm business or farmland is not matrimonial property, the obvious *esto* argument is that these assets should not be divided equally, on the basis of special circumstances.

Section 10(1) of the 1985 Act notes that the matrimonial assets shall be divided fairly when there is equal sharing, or in such proportions as are justified by special circumstances. The examples of "special circumstances" set out at section 10(6) are not exhaustive, but there are two of particular interest for farming cases. The first is section 10(6)(b), being the source of the funds used to acquire any of the matrimonial property; and the second is section 10(6)(d), being the nature and use of the matrimonial property and the extent to which it is reasonable to expect it to be realised, divided or used as security.

Specific examples of this principle being applied in farming cases are found in *Davidson v Davidson 1994 SLT 506; MacLean v MacLean 2001 FamLR 118; R v R 2000 FamLR 43* and the recent case of *Bradbury v Bradbury 2021 CSOH 113*.

In *Davidson*, the parties had bought a farm during the marriage with funds realised by the wife from her inheritance, which the wife then farmed whilst the husband worked elsewhere. It was agreed at proof that this farm was the sole matrimonial asset, and was worth

£177,000. The Court held that it was impossible not to give due weight to the fact that the farm was acquired entirely by the use of inherited funds, and that it had been used solely by the pursuer wife for the purpose of carrying on a farming business. Balanced against this were various arguments for unequal sharing in favour of the husband, resulting in an award to him of £60,000 (and so about 33% of the total matrimonial assets).

In *MacLean*, the wife was again in receipt of non-matrimonial property which had converted, resulting in an award of 25% of the total pot to the husband.

In *R v R*, the husband was the one from a farming family – land had been sold during the marriage and another farm bought, with the consequence that to a large extent, the whole net matrimonial property was derived from realisation of assets acquired by him way of succession or gift. The husband also continued to own a farm which was not matrimonial property. The Court held that *"due weight must be given to the fact that to a very large extent [the matrimonial property] derives from inherited or gifted assets which, had they not been sold, would have been outwith the scope of matrimonial property."* Again, set against other arguments for unequal sharing on behalf of the wife, sum of £380,000 was awarded to her, being about 32% of the matrimonial property.

It should be noted that all of these cases follow the trend of adopting a rather broad-brush, percentage-based split of the assets, whereas an alternative approach in the intervening years, particularly in non-farming cases, has been for the Court to identify specific assets and figures to which special circumstances could be applied. However, the case of *Bradbury v Bradbury 2021 CSOH 113* arguably reverts to a more broad-brush analysis. In that case, a pre-marital farm had been sold, with the sale proceeds used during the course of the marriage to acquire a new farm and set up a new sole trader business. The net matrimonial property was about £2.9 million. The proceeds of sale of the pre-marital farm were £2.633 million. Had full account been taken of the defender husband's "source of funds" argument, the wife would therefore have received a fairly small sum, compared to the total matrimonial pot. However, set against that was the wife's economic disadvantage argument (detailed further below). The Court noted (at para 73) that a significant impact on the expansion of the farming business should be attributed to the investment of the proceeds of sale of the original farm (a non-matrimonial asset), and that it would not be fair to divide the net matrimonial property equally. A sum of £900,000 was awarded to the wife – adding in the property and pension (totalling about £100,000) already in her name, that amounted to share of about £1 million. Given the total pot of £2.9M, the wife's claim therefore fell rather within the same percentage window as the above much earlier cases – although as this was not set out in the judgment, this may be coincidence rather than continuation of a trend.

Economic disadvantage and the burden of childcare

Whereas source of funds is the obvious argument for the farmer, economic disadvantage in terms of section 9(1)(b) is the obvious argument (or counter-argument) for the claimant.

Section 9(1)(b) must be read in conjunction with section 11(2), which directs the Court to have regard to the extent to which the economic advantages or disadvantages sustained by either person have been balanced by the economic advantages or disadvantages sustained by the other, and whether any resulting imbalance will be corrected by a sharing of the value of the matrimonial property.

Section 9(1)(c) sets out that the economic burden of caring for a child of the marriage under the age of 16 should be shared fairly between the parties, taking into account the list of factors set out in section 11(3).

One route to arguing economic disadvantage in farming cases is to set out that the claimant has done unpaid work on the farm, to the advantage of the farmer, which has prevented the claimant from advancing a separate career. A list of such work was included in *B v B 2011 FamLR 91,* being that the claimant had provided meals for temporary workers; counted ear tags on stock for Ministry visits; driven the tractor to collect trailers; lodged cheques with the firm's bank account; prepared wages; and decorated certain of the farm properties. Similarly, in *Bradbury v Bradbury 2021 CSOH 113,* the pursuer wife gave detailed evidence as to her involvement not just in care for the family, but also direct farm work, such as dosing and dipping the sheep; taking lambs to be slaughtered and butchered; labelling meat and taking it to markets; as well as renovation of farm properties and management of holiday lets. Evidence was also taken from a number of family members and employees in support of that case. It is fairly usual for the farmer to contest that this work was not in fact done by the claimant, or that the amount was much less than the claimant asserts, and that is what happened in *Bradbury*, with the husband claiming she wasn't actively involved apart from a small amount of book-keeping, and instead left him *"in the lurch"*. However, in what was described as "rigorous" cross examination, he admitted that the running of the farm business was a "joint effort", thus undermining his assertion that his wife played only a modest role. A considerable part of the judgment was taken up with assessing the credibility and reliability of the witnesses, and these very contrasting accounts, with the Court ultimately preferring the wife's evidence.

A second route into "economic disadvantage" territory is to show that there has been a significant uplift in value of a non-matrimonial asset; that this uplift stems at least in part from the contributions (financial or otherwise) of the claimant; and there would be economic advantage to the other spouse and disadvantage to the claimant if this value was not shared. A recent example of this type of s9(1)(b) argument (albeit in a non-farming case) is in *T v T 2021 CSOH 6*, where the wife had businesses stemming from before the marriage, for which the husband worked and was remunerated. Lady Wise noted that *"the legislation provides ways of dealing with property that is held in a non-matrimonial wrapper but which cannot be ignored because it represents in part or in whole the fruits of the labour of one of both of the parties during the marriage. ... The provision through which the court can take account of situations such as the one in this case is through principle 9(1)(b) of the 1985 Act."* Accordingly, an additional capital sum was awarded to take account of the economic advantage gained by the wife from the husband's very significant non-financial contributions to the companies. However, Lady Wise noted that it was surprising that the husband had not chosen to lead more detailed evidence as to the value created or gained within the companies during the marriage, especially during the years of his stewardship. In *Bradbury*, this type of evidence was led in more detail, in particular in relation to the increase in value in the first, non-matrimonial farm. As noted above, a pre-marital farm had been sold in this case, with the sale proceeds used to acquire a new farm. The wife countered the husband's "source of funds" arguments stemming from the first farm by seeking to demonstrate her considerable contribution to the increase in value of this, which was acquired in 1995 (50% by way of gift, and 50% purchased for £128,000) and sold 15 years later for over £2.6 million. The wife argued that both she and the husband had embarked on a project to improve and transform that farm, including a huge amount of work by her personally in vastly improving the farmhouse, refurbishing cottages for holiday lets, and converting a derelict barn into further properties. Lord Brailsford took into account the *"considerable economic advantage"* gained by the husband as a result of the marriage, having ended with a much larger farming enterprise than he had at the start of the marriage. Lastly, *M v S 2017 CSOH 151* is an interesting example of this type of argument in relation to contributions and increase in value of a farm, but in relation to cohabitation, rather than divorce.

The discretion exercised in terms of applying the principles in section 9(1)(b) and (c) might seem to be influenced also by the need of the claimant, in particular for housing (perhaps more along the lines of dicta about "reasonable need" from the English court). For example, in *B v B 2011 FamLR 91*, the court considered the claimant's suggestions for housing, her mortgage capacity and the maximum the husband said he could feasibly raise, before settling on the sum of £90,000 (when a half share of the matrimonial property would have been £7840), as reflecting her arguments under sections 9(1)(b) and (c), while noting that would allow her to purchase an appropriate property. In *Bradbury*, section 9(1)(c) was not relevant, but the Court still noted the wife's general intent to purchase a farm and work this with her two adult children.

As with s9(1)(b) cases in general, economic advantage/disadvantage arguments in farm case are not always wholly or even partially successful – see *M v M [2014] Fam LR 116,* where the Court noted it would be *"artificial, given the intervening period of 20 years and the vagaries of life"* to disregard the possibility that the claimant's career might not have worked out as successfully as he or she hoped; or *Johnston v Johnston 2004 Fam LB 70-6*, where the wife's assistance on the farm was found not to have resulted in any economic advantage to the husband. Economic disadvantage still remains a difficult argument to make out, even in the extremes of gifted/inherited property which can arise in farming scenarios.

CHAPTER ELEVEN

ARGUING LACK OF RESOURCES

A very significant difficulty in farming cases is how to raise the capital needed for a settlement, when most or all of the farmer's wealth is tied up in the land and business. This is an issue which both parties need to give thought to. One problem for the paying party is that lack of resources might only become clear relatively late in the negotiation process, once the difficult issues of identification and valuation of matrimonial property has taken place. Putting together a comprehensive and persuasive case regarding lack of resources can take time, and so this needs to be factored in to planning and proof / negotiation preparation.

Sale of the land

The claimant's position might be that the answer to lack of liquid resources is simple – just sell off part of the land. The farmer's rebuttal is likely to be that if that was done, the farm simply wouldn't be able to continue. The Court noted this in *B v B 2011 FamLR 91,* stating that the farm is a *"special type of business"* and that any asset disposal *"has to be carefully considered in the context of the farm's long-term viability"* (para 34). Any such argument in relation to this should be carefully evidenced – the farmer's own view on this, whilst helpful, is unlikely to be enough. *M v M [2014] CSOH 136* is a good example of the steps to go through. In that case, the claimant identified two properties which she claimed could be sold to raise funds. Both parties instructed surveyors. The defender's surveyor was of the opinion that one of the identified farm properties could not be sold without undermining the intrinsic value of the estate. With the other property, the surveyor identified issues with likely delay in obtaining vacant possession from tenants in order to allow sale. Lastly, the defender's position was that his ability to pay for the education of the parties' children was dependent on the ongoing viability of the estate, and led evidence to demonstrate that sale of properties, with the consequent drop in rental income, would compromise the overall financial position of the estate.

Other potential evidential avenues to explore might be a report from an agricultural specialist about the viability (or not) of the farm if part of it was sold off; or a view from a land valuer as to whether sale of individual plots of land would be possible (given access problems, or planning or use restrictions). An estate agent might also be able to give a view as to marketability.

A further issue with sale of land might be due to the other owners, if the farmer does not have sole ownership or control. This was another factor in *B v B,* where the court noted (para 34) that a further constraint was the attitude of the farmer's parents, given that he could not dispose of assets without their consent.

Borrowing

Financing a settlement through borrowing is a further option which the potential paying party may need to explore. In terms of the structure of any such borrowings, the simplest option would for the farmer to borrow in his/her sole name, and with any security over his/her own assets. That may however not be possible, if the farm business and assets are held jointly with others, such as siblings or parents. Any co-owners would need to give consent to borrow over an asset in which they have an interest, and should take independent legal advice in relation to the same and the structure of any borrowings.

It is important to both give clear information and receive a clear answer from any lending institution. The Court will wish sight of what information has been passed to the bank in order for a decision on lending to be made. Responses on this can also take time, and again the family lawyer should factor this in to case preparation.

If this line is to be run, detailed evidence is usually necessary, and so early thought needs to be given to this. In *Bradbury v Bradbury 2021 CSOH 113,* there was argument about whether any such resources argument could even be led, as the pursuer argued that there had been no fair notice of the same in the pleadings. While evidence on resources was permitted, the Court noted this was not detailed or comprehensive, didn't include the evidence that might have been expected from the defender's bankers, accountant or other experts in relation to raising capital, and so would not have assisted in relation to a resources argument. In contrast, in *M v M* (above) evidence was produced that the defender's current bank had rejected applications by him for further loan facilities or for increased drawings, even if security was to be made available; the defender did however advise that he was able to get lending (to a fixed ceiling, and on conditions) with an alternative institution.

CHAPTER TWELVE

DEALING WITH THE FARM PARTNERSHIP

If the spouses are partners in the farm business, it is likely that this partnership will either be brought to an end on the divorce; or one spouse will take over the other's share; or (at a minimum) there will be a significant restructuring of the partnership going forward. We will consider each of these situations in turn.

<u>Dissolution of the partnership</u>

If the partnership is to be brought to an end as a going concern, there will need to be a dissolution, followed by winding up the partnership affairs.

The specifics around the dissolution will largely depend upon what the terms of the partnership agreement are. If there is a written partnership agreement, then it is likely (but not guaranteed) that it will have provisions governing termination, in particular to provide for a notice period so as to avoid an immediate termination. If there is no alternative agreement regarding termination of the partnership, then the Partnership Act will regulate the giving of any notice of termination. Where the partnership is a partnership "at will" (i.e. not for a fixed term) termination may be effected either in terms of section 26 or section 32(1)(c) of the Act. Termination can take effect as soon as notice of termination is communicated to the other partners – and so it makes sense to consider carefully when this is to be given, and if bringing the partnership immediately to an end at that point is truly what is desired.

It is also possible to seek dissolution by order of Court in a variety of circumstances as set out in section 35 of the Act, including incapacity; where one partner has acted in a way calculated to prejudicially affect the carrying on of the business; where one partner wilfully or persistently breaches the partnership agreement or conducts themselves in a manner so that it is not reasonably practicable to carry on business; or otherwise where it is just and equitable that the partnership be dissolved.

Once dissolved, the partnership will be wound up. In terms of s38 of the Partnership Act, once the partnership is dissolved, each partner can only bind the firm so far as may be necessary to wind up the partnership affairs, or to complete any transactions begun but unfinished at the time of dissolution. Sections 39 and 44 set out the default for how the partnership property is to be distributed, being:

- losses to be paid first out of profit, then capital, then by the partners individually (per their profit sharing proportions);

- surplus assets to go first to pay the debts of non-partners, then to repay advances made by partners to the firm;

- assets then to be used to pay what each partner is due from the firm by way of capital; and

- any residue to be divided per the partner's profit-sharing proportions.

If the partnership is to be dissolved and wound up, any agreement regulating this will need to be carefully coordinated with a Minute of Agreement dealing with the remainder of the matrimonial property and claims on divorce. To ensure that all partnership claims and circumstances are properly dealt with, it will usually make sense for the dissolution/winding up to be dealt with in a separate document.

This would seem particularly necessary where the partners are not just the spouses. For clarity, that partnership document can then be referred to and included as an appendix to the Minute of Agreement, both documents being signed at the same time, as part of a comprehensive settlement of all claims, both matrimonial and relating to the partnership.

Transfer of one partner's share

If one partner is to continue in the business, then instead of a dissolution, that partner may seek transfer of the spouse's interest in the business. As noted in Chapter Seven, this can be sought as part of the divorce action.

If negotiated, then the transfer would likely be recorded in a Retirement Agreement, which would again likely be appended to and linked up with a Minute of Agreement dealing specifically with the matrimonial aspects. The Retirement Agreement can provide for whether the partnership is going to continue with the remaining partners, or whether the business will be taken forward by the other spouse as a sole trader. It can also provide for whether any consideration is to be paid to the retiring partner; whether any partnership assets are to be retained by that partner; and any indemnities or undertakings given by either partner against past or future losses or claims.

The parties and family lawyer should consider the timing of any transfer of partnership interest in the context of separation, given the capital gains tax rules allowing for such transfers between spouses on a "no gain, no loss" basis during the tax year of the separation. In order to prevent the outgoing partner from having a potential capital gains tax liability, it may make sense for that partner to retire and transfer their interest prior to the end of the tax year of separation, even if the parties have not yet reached a comprehensive settlement.

In such case, the Retirement Agreement would be linked to an Interim (not final) Minute of Agreement. The potential tax benefits of doing so obviously need to be considered and weighed against the disadvantage to that outgoing partner no longer having a stake in the business, decision-making powers or a right to drawings.

Continuation of partnership

A third option is for the partnership simply to continue with both spouses. That is a very unusual route in the context of a separation, but may be considered by a couple who believe that they can continue to work together and have sufficient incentive (whether financial or for family reasons) to make this work. If that option is possible, very careful thought will need to be given to how the business will operate, probably with a specifically tailored partnership agreement.

CHAPTER THIRTEEN

DEALING WITH FAMILY DYNAMICS

Farming is very often a family business. Sometimes, other members of the family have a legal stake in the business, as landowners, partners or shareholders. Sometimes, the younger generation has no legal interest (yet) but has an expectation or hope that the farm will one day come to them. This can often add an extra dimension to the matrimonial dispute, usually (unfortunately) by making things rather more difficult to resolve.

<u>Alignment with one spouse</u>

It is not uncommon for relatives in farming cases to align strongly with one spouse or the other. This can cause difficulties for negotiations, but also for gathering and presenting evidence. This is perhaps exemplified by the evidence given by the adult children in *Bradbury v Bradbury 2021 CSOH 113*, where the Court had to carefully consider their reliability and credibility, given their allegedly entrenched position in support of their mother and the fact that they had admitted to acts of vandalism on their father's property. Lord Brailsford noted as follows: *"I accept that I require to examine their evidence with great care. I am not however prepared to disregard their evidence as being wholly incredible because of their views relative to their father or to their conduct in wilfully damaging his property."*

Conflict issues

If other family members (whether parents, siblings or adult children) are legally involved in the farm business, their interests will be affected one way or another by the divorce, perhaps due to one spouse leaving the business, or the farm partnership being dissolved or wound up. In such a case, that family member's interest may benefit from legal representation also. That may need to be separate legal representation, if there is an actual or potential conflict of interest between the spouse and the other family member.

A family-based solution?

An alternative, and perhaps more positive, result of the farming family dynamic is if both spouses agree that they want the farm to remain in the family, and are prepared to work together to ensure that outcome. This may mean moving away from a court-imposed solution, given that the Court is restricted to the factors and orders set out in the 1985 Act, and instead considering alternative dispute resolution options. Mediation, in particular, can allow such hope and intent to be expressed (in a safe space), considered and potentially taken into account, with the option to discuss and implement more innovative and bespoke solutions.

This might translate to one party not insisting on a full share of the assets, if that means the farm can be passed down intact to the next generation. It could also result in a division which passes assets directly to that next generation now, perhaps with a liferent or other minimal interest retained by the spouse – clearly, the spouse needs to be very certain that they do in fact wish to give up their rights in this way.

An alternative approach is to seek to agree that farm assets be distributed to family in a particular way following death. It is possible for a party to bind the other to the effect that the latter loses the power to revoke a will in situations where a contract has been entered into during lifetime, with the old case of *Paterson v Paterson (1893) 20 R. 484* being an example of this. Although this option has the benefit of not giving away assets immediately, it is a very considerable restriction on testamentary intent, may have adverse consequences on inheritance tax planning, and accordingly may simply store up problems (and legal debate and cost) for another day.

CHAPTER FOURTEEN

PREVENTATIVE STEPS

In the thick of a difficult separation, many farming couples will wish that they had taken legal advice at a much earlier stage, to clarify the confusion of a farm partnership formed by a handshake rather than a well-drafted document, or where it is entirely unclear who owns the land, or where (unknown to the recipient) conversion has turned gifts and inheritances into matrimonial property. Hindsight is a wonderful thing, but legal and financial advisors have the benefit of seeing the same situations again and again, and so are best-placed to steer clients away from the mistakes others have made previously.

There are different methods farming couples can use to provide both clarity and protection.

Pre-nuptial agreement

Many family law clients routinely underestimate how difficult the process of obtaining a pre-nuptial agreement can be. It is not simply an off-the-shelf piece of paper where the appropriate box is ticked and the document signed. Instead, the couple need to be able to consider a number of different and complex things: firstly, emotionally contemplating a difficult separation from the person whom they currently love best in the world; then, getting to grips with the default law which might apply if they separate without having an agreement in place, whether a short period after the wedding or decades in the future; understanding issues of enforceability; thinking about what they want the agreement to actually say; and doing all of that in the busy and perhaps stressful period leading up to the wedding date. This is perhaps harder to contemplate for a farmer who may well be in a situation where the farm business has operated for decades without any "need" for a written document or legal drafting. It can all seem too difficult and overly complicated to go through, and be either left for another day, or just not pursued at all.

For those who leave it to one side, a post-nuptial agreement can be a good way forward, to be done at a more leisurely pace. The risk of delay until after the wedding is of course that the document never gets completed at all – a real risk when dealing with a farming family who have a thousand tasks which rank higher than speaking to a lawyer about something which seems rather complex and unpleasant. The task for the lawyer is therefore to explain the benefits and risks, so that the farming client can make an informed choice about proceeding or not; and to keep both the drafting and the process as clear and streamlined as possible.

There is a general acceptance amongst family law practitioners that pre- and post-nups are likely treated as binding in Scots law. However, this is not something which has been thoroughly tested in reported case law. Given the agreement will be relied upon in the future, how the law may develop (and so how effective the document might be) cannot be guaranteed.

A pre-nuptial agreement may be set aside due to contractual issues (e.g. fraud; facility and circumvention; undue influence; error; misrepresentation etc), or in terms of section 16(1)(b) of the 1985 Act, which allows the court to set aside or vary an agreement if this was not fair or reasonable at the time it was entered into. The principles to take into account when considering section 16(1)(b) are stated in *Gillon v Gillon (No 3) 1995 S.L.T. 678,* as well as *Bradley v Bradley [2017] SAC (Civ) 29.*

It is usual in a Scottish pre-nuptial agreement to ring-fence non-matrimonial property, and this would seem of very clear benefit in a farming scenario with gifted or inherited or pre-marriage assets. It is possible to go further, whether by guaranteeing a certain level of provision for the claimant spouse; or indicating that neither party will make any claims at all on separation. However, the further the parties move away from the provisions of the 1985 Act, the greater the risk that an agreement might be seen as not fair and reasonable.

If the parties do not wish to enter into a pre- or post-nuptial agreement, a lesser option may be to detail a clear record of gifts, so that there is no confusion or ambiguity in the future about the fact that farm assets have been gifted, rather than acquired for value. This will not protect against conversion to matrimonial property in the same way that a pre-nuptial agreement would, but at least clarifies the fact of the gift itself.

Partnership Agreement

If the partnership has subsisted entirely via an oral agreement, or a written agreement which is poorly drafted and unsatisfactory, marriage can be a prompt to consider what fresh written agreement can better replace these.

The process of considering the partnership agreement can promote future-focussed thinking between the partners, which in itself can be very helpful. The document can cover a multitude of matters, and be as bespoke as the couple wish, including how profits will be shared (equally or otherwise); how decisions will be taken; and importantly on what basis and how the partnership will be dissolved.

CHAPTER FIFTEEN

TIPS FOR FARM ADVISERS

The farm accountant and adviser is often well-placed to help guide a farming client, but (as the Scottish farmer-poet wrote) best-laid plans gang aft agley. One way this can often happen is a change made to the farm business, often with the best of intent, which has disastrous and unforeseen implications on separation. So what can the farm adviser do to avoid this?

<u>Phone a friend</u>

Often, the ill-effects of changes could be avoided if the adviser had asked the question: "*So, how is your marriage?*" Tax savings and benefits from re-arranging the business which would be entirely sensible if things are solid on the matrimonial front easily slide into very poor planning if the relationship is on the rocks.

The accountant may feel ill-equipped or awkward in having this sort of blunt conversation. In this case, one option is to send your client to a family lawyer instead, for a chat through the implications of the proposed change (bearing in mind that due to conflict rules, the lawyer can only advise one of the parties, not the couple together). The family lawyer will be rather more used to poking inside personal issues, and can give legal advice on the worst case scenarios. As noted in Chapter Fourteen, a pre- or post-nuptial agreement might be a sensible way forward – but even if the client decides this is not for them, at least they will have done so on a fully informed basis.

Think about the land

As will be evident from Chapter Six, a very complex question is whether or not the land is held within the partnership, or separately by one or both spouses. This is a question which can have a huge impact on the financial outcome of separation. The accountant can ensure that this is thought-through, rather than causing potential problems down the line by entering land on the balance sheet of accounts without query, or simply because that's what the previous firm of accountants did. Does the client truly understand how the land is held, together with all of the implications of that? The accountant's work, whether dealing with the balance sheet, or the partners' capital accounts, or preparing a note of assets for a lender, can have significant impact – has the accountant considered how their work could affect the business, the partnership property and the future matrimonial property, one way or another?

A cautionary note is apparent from much of the case law, but one case to highlight in particular is the English one of *Ham v Bell [2016] EWHC 1791 (CH)*, and in particular the comment at para 63 that *"accountants often overlook or misunderstand the true meaning of the word 'capital'. Thus the appearance of the value of an asset in the accounts and in one of more of the partners' capital accounts does not necessarily signify an agreement that it is partnership property"*. That lack of clarity about whether or not this appearance meant the land was partnership property was, unfortunately, one of the triggers for a four-year litigation between a farming son and his parents, during the course of which the father passed away and the litigation was conducted by his executors. If farm advisers or accountants prompted clear and purposeful discussion of exactly what is partnership property, and exactly what should be within the accounts, this might avoid similar situations arising in the future.

Be careful with language

Further risks about the future consequences of farm advice is set out in *Bradbury v Bradbury 2021 CSOH 113,* described more fully in Chapter Ten. A major part of the case centred around the wife's claim for "economic disadvantage", and whether her evidence (that she had done very extensive work on the farm) or the husband's evidence (that she had done very little) should be preferred. The business was a sole trader, in the husband's name. One piece of evidence taken into account was that the farm accountant had prepared a brief for bank loan funding some years before the separation, discussed and approved by the husband, in which it was stated that he *"farms in partnership with his wife".* The Court considered whether that statement might be false, and intended, in some way, to make the brief more attractive to the bank. However, taking into account all of the other evidence, the Court held that the statement in the funding brief was a true recollection of the factual nature of the spouses' working relationship – thus sounding a warning call to accountants and farm advisers of the potential future consequences of their drafting, and the need to be absolutely precise and accurate.

Ensure gifts remain gifts

Many advisors will be involved in the planning and logistics of passing the farm onto the next generation. This will often involve parents transferring the farmland into their adult child's name. Farmland which a farmer spouse receives by way of gift from his/her parents during the marriage is not matrimonial property and will remain ring-fenced if the farmer spouse continues to hold it in their sole name. Accordingly, it is crucial that gifts are given outright and that no consideration is paid directly or indirectly to the parents – otherwise, it will be open to the other spouse to argue that the farmland was acquired for value rather than gifted and that it therefore constitutes matrimonial property.

One way to help avoid ambiguity is to ensure that the disposition transferring farmland is for "love favour and affection" rather than for consideration and that the LBTT submission receipt on the disposition also records that the transfer is a gift.

Consideration can however be present in a more roundabout way. Think twice about creating a loan account as a tax efficient way of income being paid to the parents following transfer of the farmland – it could be argued this is consideration for the land. It may also be best to avoid any arrangement whereby the parents continue to receive any benefit from the business – e.g. by remain living in the property they have gifted for less than market-rent, or receiving a monthly "pension" from the business. Aside from any potential tax issues arising from the above, these could amount to "consideration", meaning that the asset will not have been gifted and could be held to be matrimonial property and in the pot for sharing. If there is any lack of clarity about potential conversion of a gift/inheritance to matrimonial property, could a pre- or post-nuptial agreement, or a new or refreshed partnership agreement help to correct that?

Tax isn't everything

Farmers are often given advice in order to reduce their tax liability, without detailed consideration being given to the impact those decisions could have on marital separation.

They will often be advised to bring their spouse in as a partner, transfer assets to a spouse or to form a new partnership – all of which can have beneficial tax consequences, and so might save money in the short-term. But by doing any of these things, the farmer may be inadvertently converting previously ring-fenced non-matrimonial property (which would not have entered the pot for sharing on divorce) into matrimonial property (which will enter the pot to be shared on divorce).

Advisers and accountants need to consider the potential long-term implications of such decisions, rather than just the short-term tax gain – and as above, send their client for family law advice if uncertain.

MORE BOOKS BY LAW BRIEF PUBLISHING

A selection of our other titles available now:-

'A Practical Guide to Transgender Law' by Robin Moira White & Nicola Newbegin
'Artificial Intelligence – The Practical Legal Issues (2nd Edition)' by John Buyers
'A Practical Guide to Challenging Sham Marriage Allegations in Immigration Law' by Priya Solanki
'A Practical Guide to New Build Conveyancing' by Paul Sams & Rebecca East
'A Practical Guide to Inherited Wealth on Divorce' by Hayley Trim
'A Practical Guide to Shareholder Disputes in Family Businesses' by Ed Weeks
'A Practical Guide to the Law of Forests in Scotland' by Philip Buchan
'A Practical Guide to Health and Medical Cases in Immigration Law' by Rebecca Chapman & Miranda Butler
'A Practical Guide to Bad Character Evidence for Criminal Practitioners by Aparna Rao
'A Practical Guide to Environmental Enforcement' by Christopher Badger & Stuart Jessop
'A Practical Guide to Hoarding and Mental Health for Housing Lawyers' by Rachel Coyle
'A Practical Guide to Psychiatric Claims in Personal Injury – 2nd Edition' by Liam Ryan
'Stephens on Contractual Indemnities' by Richard Stephens
'A Practical Guide to the EU Succession Regulation' by Richard Frimston
'A Practical Guide to Solicitor and Client Costs – 2nd Edition' by Robin Dunne
'Constructive Dismissal – Practice Pointers and Principles' by Benjimin Burgher
'A Practical Guide to Religion and Belief Discrimination Claims in the Workplace' by Kashif Ali
'A Practical Guide to the Law of Medical Treatment Decisions' by Ben Troke

'Fundamental Dishonesty and QOCS in Personal Injury Proceedings: Law and Practice' by Jake Rowley
'A Practical Guide to the Law in Relation to School Exclusions' by Charlotte Hadfield & Alice de Coverley
'A Practical Guide to Divorce for the Silver Separators' by Karin Walker
'The Right to be Forgotten – The Law and Practical Issues' by Melissa Stock
'A Practical Guide to Planning Law and Rights of Way in National Parks, the Broads and AONBs' by James Maurici QC, James Neill et al
'A Practical Guide to Election Law' by Tom Tabori
'A Practical Guide to the Law in Relation to Surrogacy' by Andrew Powell
'A Practical Guide to Claims Arising from Fatal Accidents – 2nd Edition' by James Patience
'A Practical Guide to the Ownership of Employee Inventions – From Entitlement to Compensation' by James Tumbridge & Ashley Roughton
'A Practical Guide to Asbestos Claims' by Jonathan Owen & Gareth McAloon
'A Practical Guide to Stamp Duty Land Tax in England and Northern Ireland' by Suzanne O'Hara
'A Practical Guide to the Law of Farming Partnerships' by Philip Whitcomb
'Covid-19, Homeworking and the Law – The Essential Guide to Employment and GDPR Issues' by Forbes Solicitors
'Covid-19, Force Majeure and Frustration of Contracts – The Essential Guide' by Keith Markham
'Covid-19 and Criminal Law – The Essential Guide' by Ramya Nagesh
'Covid-19 and Family Law in England and Wales – The Essential Guide' by Safda Mahmood
'A Practical Guide to the Law of Unlawful Eviction and Harassment – 2nd Edition' by Stephanie Lovegrove
'Covid-19, Residential Property, Equity Release and Enfranchisement – The Essential Guide' by Paul Sams and Louise Uphill
'Covid-19, Brexit and the Law of Commercial Leases – The Essential Guide' by Mark Shelton
'A Practical Guide to Costs in Personal Injury Claims – 2nd Edition' by Matthew Hoe

'A Practical Guide to the General Data Protection Regulation (GDPR) – 2nd Edition' by Keith Markham
'Ellis on Credit Hire – Sixth Edition' by Aidan Ellis & Tim Kevan
'A Practical Guide to Working with Litigants in Person and McKenzie Friends in Family Cases' by Stuart Barlow
'Protecting Unregistered Brands: A Practical Guide to the Law of Passing Off' by Lorna Brazell
'A Practical Guide to Secondary Liability and Joint Enterprise Post-Jogee' by Joanne Cecil & James Mehigan
'A Practical Guide to the Pre-Action RTA Claims Protocol for Personal Injury Lawyers' by Antonia Ford
'A Practical Guide to Neighbour Disputes and the Law' by Alexander Walsh
'A Practical Guide to Forfeiture of Leases' by Mark Shelton
'A Practical Guide to Coercive Control for Legal Practitioners and Victims' by Rachel Horman
'A Practical Guide to Rights Over Airspace and Subsoil' by Daniel Gatty
'Tackling Disclosure in the Criminal Courts – A Practitioner's Guide' by Narita Bahra QC & Don Ramble
'A Practical Guide to the Law of Driverless Cars – Second Edition' by Alex Glassbrook, Emma Northey & Scarlett Milligan
'A Practical Guide to TOLATA Claims' by Greg Williams
'A Practical Guide to Elderly Law – 2nd Edition' by Justin Patten
'A Practical Guide to the Law of Prescription in Scotland' by Andrew Foyle
'A Practical Guide to the Construction and Rectification of Wills and Trust Instruments' by Edward Hewitt
'A Practical Guide to the Law of Bullying and Harassment in the Workplace' by Philip Hyland
'How to Be a Freelance Solicitor: A Practical Guide to the SRA-Regulated Freelance Solicitor Model' by Paul Bennett
'A Practical Guide to Prison Injury Claims' by Malcolm Johnson
'A Practical Guide to the Small Claims Track - 2nd Edition' by Dominic Bright
'A Practical Guide to Advising Clients at the Police Station' by Colin Stephen McKeown-Beaumont

'A Practical Guide to Antisocial Behaviour Injunctions' by Iain Wightwick

'Practical Mediation: A Guide for Mediators, Advocates, Advisers, Lawyers, and Students in Civil, Commercial, Business, Property, Workplace, and Employment Cases' by Jonathan Dingle with John Sephton

'The Mini-Pupillage Workbook' by David Boyle

'A Practical Guide to Crofting Law' by Brian Inkster

'A Practical Guide to Spousal Maintenance' by Liz Cowell

'A Practical Guide to the Law of Domain Names and Cybersquatting' by Andrew Clemson

'A Practical Guide to the Law of Gender Pay Gap Reporting' by Harini Iyengar

'A Practical Guide to the Rights of Grandparents in Children Proceedings' by Stuart Barlow

'NHS Whistleblowing and the Law' by Joseph England

'Employment Law and the Gig Economy' by Nigel Mackay & Annie Powell

'A Practical Guide to Noise Induced Hearing Loss (NIHL) Claims' by Andrew Mckie, Ian Skeate, Gareth McAloon

'An Introduction to Beauty Negligence Claims – A Practical Guide for the Personal Injury Practitioner' by Greg Almond

'Intercompany Agreements for Transfer Pricing Compliance' by Paul Sutton

'Zen and the Art of Mediation' by Martin Plowman

'A Practical Guide to the SRA Principles, Individual and Law Firm Codes of Conduct 2019 – What Every Law Firm Needs to Know' by Paul Bennett

'A Practical Guide to Adoption for Family Lawyers' by Graham Pegg

'A Practical Guide to Industrial Disease Claims' by Andrew Mckie & Ian Skeate

'A Practical Guide to Redundancy' by Philip Hyland

'A Practical Guide to Vicarious Liability' by Mariel Irvine

'A Practical Guide to Applications for Landlord's Consent and Variation of Leases' by Mark Shelton

'A Practical Guide to Relief from Sanctions Post-Mitchell and Denton' by Peter Causton

'A Practical Guide to Equity Release for Advisors' by Paul Sams

'A Practical Guide to Financial Services Claims' by Chris Hegarty

'The Law of Houses in Multiple Occupation: A Practical Guide to HMO Proceedings' by Julian Hunt
'Occupiers, Highways and Defective Premises Claims: A Practical Guide Post-Jackson – 2nd Edition' by Andrew Mckie
'A Practical Guide to Financial Ombudsman Service Claims' by Adam Temple & Robert Scrivenor
'A Practical Guide to Advising Schools on Employment Law' by Jonathan Holden
'A Practical Guide to Running Housing Disrepair and Cavity Wall Claims: 2nd Edition' by Andrew Mckie & Ian Skeate
'A Practical Guide to Holiday Sickness Claims – 2nd Edition' by Andrew Mckie & Ian Skeate
'Arguments and Tactics for Personal Injury and Clinical Negligence Claims' by Dorian Williams
'A Practical Guide to Drone Law' by Rufus Ballaster, Andrew Firman, Eleanor Clot
'A Practical Guide to Compliance for Personal Injury Firms Working With Claims Management Companies' by Paul Bennett
'RTA Allegations of Fraud in a Post-Jackson Era: The Handbook – 2nd Edition' by Andrew Mckie
'RTA Personal Injury Claims: A Practical Guide Post-Jackson' by Andrew Mckie
'On Experts: CPR35 for Lawyers and Experts' by David Boyle
'An Introduction to Personal Injury Law' by David Boyle
'A Practical Guide to Subtle Brain Injury Claims' by Pankaj Madan

These books and more are available to order online direct from the publisher at www.lawbriefpublishing.com, where you can also read free sample chapters. For any queries, contact us on 0844 587 2383 or mail@lawbriefpublishing.com.

Our books are also usually in stock at www.amazon.co.uk with free next day delivery for Prime members, and at good legal bookshops such as Wildy & Sons.

We are regularly launching new books in our series of practical day-to-day practitioners' guides. Visit our website and join our free newsletter to be kept informed and to receive special offers, free chapters, etc.

You can also follow us on Twitter at www.twitter.com/lawbriefpub.